with best wishes
Jenny Ward

The Yellow Pimpernel

A Cornish Florilegium
by
Jenny Ward

A record
by
botanical illustration
of the plants found growing in
a specific Geographical location
between July 2007 and July 2009.
Published by Jenny Ward

The Yellow Pimpernel © Jenny Ward 2010

Front cover photograph © David Kingdon
Author photograph © Charles Francis

All Botanical paintings, all other artwork, all other photographs and all text © Jenny Ward

All rights reserved. No part of this work may be photocopied, stored in a retrieval system, published, adapted, broadcast, transmitted, recorded or produced in any form or by any means without prior permission of the copyright owner.

Enquiries should be addressed to the publisher:- Jenny Ward, Menna Farm, Menna, Grampound Road, Truro, Cornwall. TR2 4HA United Kingdom

Hard back. ISBN 978-0-9567539-0-8

A CIP catalogue record of this book is available from the British Library

Printed and bound by R Booth Ltd, The Praze, Penryn, Cornwall. TR10 8AA

Published by Jenny Ward

Acknowledgements

The Author is indebted to the following for their help and encouragement during the preparation of this book:-

Christine Kingdon and David Kingdon
Keith Spurgin and Selina Bates
Charles and Mally Francis and the Tuesday group
Jacqueline Wall (Cornwall Council)
The 'Q' Fund for a grant of £250.00
Howard Curnow (Cornwall Wildlife Trust)
JLS Framing for high resolution reproductions of the original artwork
(Print reproductions of the botanical plates are available on Giclee archival papers using Epson Ultrachrome inks)
Enquiries to:- Jenny Ward, Menna Farm, Menna, Grampound Road, Truro, Cornwall, TR2 4HA.

- This book is dedicated to my family -

- with love -

---☆---

---☆---

Sunbeams dance 'cross a sheltered dell

abutting the common, close by the well.

---☆---

Fallen willows with mossy boughs

make rubbing posts for browsing cows.

---☆---

Leaf mould and bog squelch under boot

Home of the Fern and Nightshade root

Foreword

Although their interests and techniques may be quite different, botanists and painters do share an essential skill – the ability to closely observe their subjects; and these delightful paintings demonstrate what beauty there is to find in the natural world that flourishes all around us, if only we can take the time to stop and look for it. Jenny Ward has done this, and has brought the results of her study to life for us; the fading to red and yellow of the Hawthorn as the fruit ripens, Tar Spot fungus on Sycamore leaves and the slender awns of the Brome-grass – finely painted in two senses of the word. The farmer's friends are displayed: Rye-grasses for fodder, the leaning Oak that for so long supported a gate, and (reaching back further into the past), those once-useful plants: Self-heal, Groundsel, Cleavers, Rushes and Nettles. These are native species of fields, hedgerows, streams and disturbed ground, habitats where occasional newcomers have settled in, Cherry Laurel, Lesser Periwinkle and Pink-sorrel, along with Sweet Violet, a borderline species that has been recorded both as a wild plant and as an escape – or relic of cultivation.

These paintings give us information that photographs often lack, and can also reveal the spirit of a living form not always evoked by even the most skilful botanical drawing. They are the essence of a plant, conveyed by the eye to the mind of the artist, to the hand that paints, and to the eye – and finally to the mind – of the observer. Meanwhile the names of plants remind us of the seasons, especially spring, when Cuckooflower, Lords-and-ladies and Sweet Vernal-grass begin to stir. They recall former uses (Tutsan, Scurvy-grass, Woundwort, Bedstraw); and reveal the roots of our language, like Sallow, from the French Saule and Latin Salix; while familiar animals assume a different form, in Cat's-ear, Dog Rose, the diminutive Toad Rush, and Foxtail.

We are also shown the range and subtlety of the artist's palette, Yellow Bartsia, Red Campion (though most would say a shade of pink) and all the white, blues, greens and purples of the Cornish countryside – looking, in early summer, like a medieval tapestry. Jenny Ward's flowers of the field have been identified and painted within such a short space of time and with such accuracy that we can only be amazed at the skill she has displayed, both as artist and botanist. I am very happy to be able to introduce to the reader such a work, that invites us to share the joy of discovery and the celebration of natural beauty.

Keith Spurgin

Truro

18th October 2010

Introduction

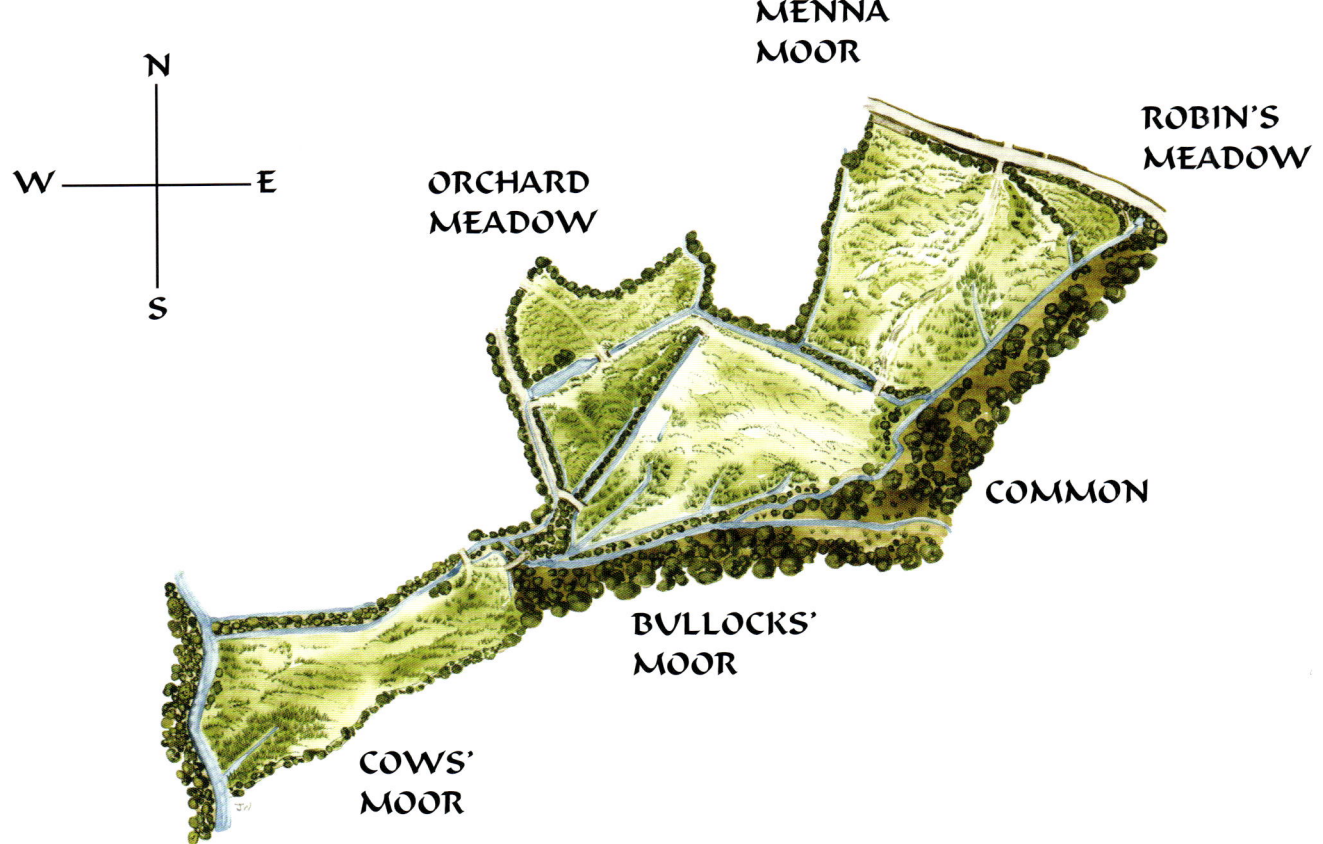

Somewhere in the catchment area of the Tresillian River is a moor. It is about 900 metres in length, 150 metres in width and 30 acres (12 hectares) in extent. A line through the centre runs from about 250 feet above sea level in the North-East to 190 feet above sea level in the South-West, where its waters drain into a tributary of the Tresillian River. The nearby Goss Moor, now a National Nature Reserve, is the largest surviving remnant of the Mid-Cornwall Moors. The subject of my study is a much smaller, but no less valuable, pocket of Mid-Cornwall Moor.

It is a wonderfully private place. At first glance it seems an unprepossessing tract of rush-infested, badly drained, unproductive pasture to be dismissed without a second thought. But only stop and look closer. Owing to the springs and the ancient hedges and ditches that surround the fields, it provides a number of different habitats in which a wide range of plants can flourish. Only to the persistent and keen-eyed observer will it reveal its hidden treasures and in so doing be transformed into a place of unique beauty and enchantment.

South Devon cattle, Menna Moor.

It has been farmed in the traditional way, now by the fifth generation of the family, as part of a 300 acre mixed farm raising beef cattle and sheep. The 30 acres comprises three main enclosures, namely; Menna Moor, Bullocks' Moor and Cows' Moor. These with two smaller enclosures; Orchard Meadow and Robin's Meadow were cultivated during the Second World War. After the war they reverted to permanent pasture which is grazed by the local breed of beef cattle, that is, the South Devon, well known for its succulent beef and docile temperament. Grazing is restricted to the period between May and October in recognition of the nature of the ground. In recent years it has been managed under the rules of the Entry Level Countryside Stewardship Scheme.

Of all the influences which have shaped my life, the pull of the land and the need to be rooted in a place is very strong and probably came from my Mother. Her Father farmed at Crossrig Farm, Morland, Penrith. She loved the farm and the stud of Clydesdale horses. Although being married to a country Doctor was a very different life, she retained a lifelong interest in farming and horses. I know she was saddened, in 2001, by the ravages of Foot and Mouth disease in that area of Cumbria or Westmorland as she knew it. My artistic traits probably came from my Father. His Mother and Sister painted. One of my Sisters painted and my Daughter and Son show artistic talents.

In life you have to make choices. When I married a farmer and put down roots in Cornwall, I chose to be fully involved in the daily work of the farm. In spite of this, the artistic side of my character was not totally extinguished by the farming years. I painted farm signs, show boxes and produced hand-lettered prize cards for The South Devon Herd Book Society's bull sales. Mostly, however, I painted doors, windows, walls, gutters and gates. Creosote and red oxide were my preferred mediums.

Turnip House, Menna Farm.

When I reached the age of 65 I made another choice. I retired from full time farm work and was able to realise a long held ambition to paint. For two years I attended classes run by Truro College. I also completed a G.C.S.E. in Fine Arts at St. Austell College gaining an A* grade. A change of direction took me to the Saw-Pit Studio, Heligan Manor and Mally Francis, tutor of botanical painting. Mally, as chairman and founder member of The Eden Project Florilegium Society (E.P.F.S.), encouraged me to submit five botanical paintings for assessment by a panel of botanists and botanical artists. I was accepted as a painting member in January 2006. Since then I have contributed to the Eden Archive which exists to record the plants of the Eden Project by botanical illustration.

There followed a period of learning which still continues. I joined the Society for All Artists (S.A.A.) and won my first prize, a voucher for art materials. The competition to grow and then paint larkspurs suited me perfectly. This gave me the confidence to apply for an S.A.A. Bursary, more in hope than expectation. Astonishingly, this bid was successful. Each member of the E.P.F.S. benefited by receiving a selection of water colour papers suitable for botanical illustration.

When Winsor and Newton introduced their new colour (Opera Rose) they ran a competition in which the new colour had to be incorporated into a painting. So I entered, submitting a further copy of the 'Sweet Potato' now in the Eden Archive. I was lucky enough to win second prize, thereby acquiring a quantity of their miniature Sable brushes.

The tradition of collecting and observing nature goes back a long way in my family. I remember as a small child, my Mother taking my sisters and me on a long trek across Salisbury Plain to see a Bee Orchid. I grew up in the shadow of Stonehenge and after completing my 'O' Levels, I was urged to do a project of my choice to keep me occupied until the end of term. I knew at once what I would do. I would record and paint the flowers of the Plain. An indication of my enthusiasm was the one and only school prize I was ever awarded.

'Sisters At Stonehenge'

A watercolour by the Author
taken from a black and white photo, circa 1941.
Painted in the style of John Constable
for G.C.S.E. coursework 2004.

The trigger for my own personal florilegium of the plants of a specific geographical location came when Keith Spurgin gave the members of the E.P.F.S. a talk on the wild flowers of Cornwall. Keith, a former Recorder for the Botanical Society of the British Isles, has spent thirty-plus years studying the wild plants of Cornwall. Keith Spurgin and Selina Bates are Authors of 'Stars In The Grass', the story of Cornish Naturalist Frederick Hamilton Davey 1868-1915.

Now, fast-forward to July 2007. After Keith's inspirational talk the germ of an idea came to me. I would record and paint the plants of the moor. The feeling of déjà vu left me slightly stunned. I dusted off my old school project and studied my earliest water-colours. Now fifty-plus years later I was ready to do it all over again. Now I had the time and I had enough skill to attempt something so challenging.

I began a field study during the wettest June/July on record. It had been too wet to turn cattle out onto these low lying moors. Therefore the pasture had been neither poached nor grazed. Cattle in these conditions would be said to have 'five mouths'. Their feet would have done much damage. The growth was phenomenal. The first problem I encountered was just physically covering the waterlogged ground.

I divided the area into the different habitats as I saw them and recorded everything in each block. I had been familiar with these fields for fifty years and was confident that I knew what grew there. How wrong I was!

Between 16th July and 8th August 2007 I recorded 140 plants. Later, between January and July 2008, I recorded a further 60 plants which were not evident or observed the previous year. Still later, in the spring of 2009, my total reached 209.

For five generations, the Family have been custodians
of this small pocket of Mid-Cornwall moor.
To discover such biodiversity in a farmed environment,
was immensely gratifying.

Having recorded them, all I had to do was paint them. I mean, how hard could it be? Obviously there were frustrations and disappointments. There were also moments of pure joy. The overall benefits to me were enormous. My horizons expanded in ways I couldn't have imagined. I kept *fit*. I learnt so much about so many things and I had *fun*. I felt as though I had been on an epic voyage of discovery which had lasted for two years and the beauty of it was I had done it without ever leaving home.

---☆---

---☆---

Water on Stone. Destined to travel

over a magic mosaic of gravel.

---☆---

So light and bright, so clean and clear,

A painter's palette of pigments' here.

---☆---

Yellow Ochre and Gamboge Hue,

Burnt Sienna and Cobalt Blue.

July 2007

Plate 1
1. Apium nodiflorum (L.) Lag. –
Fool's-water-cress
2. Veronica beccabunga L. –
Brooklime
3. Lysimachia nemorum L. –
Yellow Pimpernel

The Yellow Pimpernel was the first of many treasures I never knew existed on the farm. I picked a minute piece, rooting at a node, with one flower and made a very tentative start. After painting it, I planted the tiny stem in a seed tray and placed it against a north facing wall, where it received all the rain off the shed roof. It quickly filled the tray, went over the side and rooted in the path. It flowered continuously through the winter and was soon occupying an area of about two square metres, showing what wild plants are capable of if given some encouragement.

This first painting was followed by the Brooklime and to complete the page, the water-cress. Only after painting the latter and checking the identification did I realise that it wasn't proper water-cress. It is well named Fool's-water-cress. Only then did the magnitude of the task ahead begin to dawn.

Water-cress Corner - Bullocks' Moor

August 2007

Plate 2
1. Hypericum undulatum
Schousb. Ex Willd. –
Wavy St John's-wort
2. Ranunculus flammula L. –
Lesser Spearwort
3. Prunella vulgaris L. –
Selfheal

Bullocks' Moor looking N.E.

At the beginning I had to decide on the format. I chose Fabriano, 140lb, hot pressed, traditional white, water colour paper. The pad was twelve inches by eighteen inches. I cut two inches off the eighteen using the strip for colour testing. I left a border of 1¼ inches all around. All plants were painted life-size and knowing the above dimensions, their size can be calculated even when the image is reduced.

All were done in portrait format. None of the plants was overlapped, making it easier to reproduce them individually at a later date. I decided on groups of three. This became as many as eight of the small plants.

I enjoyed the design element involved in making a satisfying composition. I aimed to give the natural forms life and movement while still making them recognisable and showing their character. I paid particular attention to the negative shapes and the points where stems crossed.

It was a steep learning curve. I painted two pieces of Selfheal which balances the composition but soon decided that one example of each would have to suffice.

The compositions did become easier with time and practice.

September 2007

Plate 3
1. **Hypericum androsaemum** L. –
Tutsan
2. **Isolepis cernua** (Vahl) Roem. & Schult. –
Slender Club-rush
3. **Wahlenbergia hederacea** (L.) Rchb. –
Ivy-leaved Bellflower
4. **Potentilla erecta** Raeusch. –
Tormentil

The identification of the plants was a challenge. I studied as many reference books as possible. Some were better for close-ups, some for written descriptions and some for habit of growth. Not one of them told me the whole story. On many an evening I fell asleep turning the pages of flower books. Eventually the relentless drip-drip of information paid off. As facts began to sink in, the moments of enlightenment became more frequent. I relied heavily on the following books:-

The Wild Flower Key - Francis Rose. ISBN 10-7232-5175-4
In it, the Ivy-leaved Bellflower is listed as an ancient woodland indicator plant and near-threatened which makes it a bit special.

The Wild Flowers Of The British Isles - I. Garrard and D. Streeter. ISBN 0-333-32679-2
I borrowed this from the public library for long periods and found the illustrations very clear.

Concise British Flora - W. Keble Martin ISBN 0-7221-0503-7
This gift from my daughter-in-law, Sandra, who had two copies, was consulted on a daily basis.

Cassell's Wild Flowers of Britain and Northern Europe - C. Grey Wilson and M. Blamey. ISBN 0-304-36214-x
Marjorie Blamey had been an inspiration to me ever since seeing an early exhibition of her work at the Truro Christmas Fat Stock Show in the Old City Hall.

Grasses - C.E. Hubbard, Illustrations by Joan Sampson. Penguin Books, first published September 1954
This book is my grass Bible.

The Fern Guide - James Merryweather. ISBN 978-185153-228-5. Published by the Field Studies Council.
I ordered it by phone one day and it arrived the next day! It was put to use immediately.

September 2007

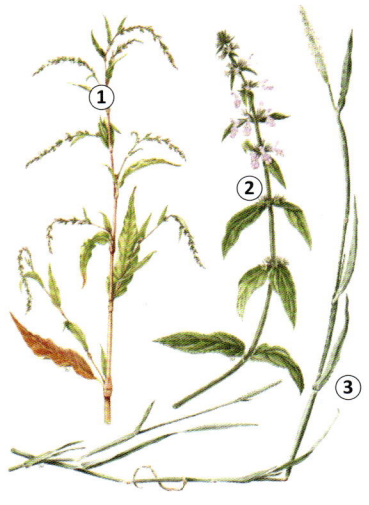

Plate 4
1. **Persicaria hydropiper** (L.) Delarbe – *Water-pepper*
2. **Stachys palustris** L. – *Marsh Woundwort*
3. **Alopecurus geniculatus** L. – *Marsh Foxtail*

As one example of the minefield that is "correct" identification, I discovered a clump of Marsh Woundwort growing profusely in one of our other fields. Being closer to hand I thought I would take a shortcut instead of going to the moor location. On closer inspection, I found it had short upper leaf stalks, whereas the upper leaves of the Marsh Woundwort are stalkless. Also, it was growing in the same habitat as the Hedge Woundwort and not in the very wet ground favoured by the Marsh Woundwort. I came to the conclusion that it was the hybrid between the two. That is, Stachys x ambigua. I had almost been taken in by its large size and luxuriant growth, which can also be a feature of the hybrid.

The lane looking North overhung by Hazel, Holly and Willow.

October 2007

Plate 5
1. **Quercus robur** L. – *Pedunculate Oak*
2. **Prunus spinosa** L. – *Blackthorn*
3. **Crataegus monogyna** Jacq. – *Hawthorn*

Only a small aspect of a large hedgerow tree can be shown, but one which confirms its identity. The hedges surrounding the moor are not hedges in the accepted sense of the word, but Cornish hedges. Cornish hedges can be stone hedges or turf hedges. The ones in the moor are a combination of the two, some places being faced with stone, others not.

They must all surely be man-made, formed over the years from soil and sub-soil dug out of the ditches. They often reach epic proportions, supporting great oak and beech trees. The ditches often run along both sides, leaving them marooned as a corridor of drier ground. The hedge-face, depending on its aspect and the amount of shade cast by the trees above, supports other diverse habitats. It is the vegetation with its intertwining root systems that keeps the hedge from falling down. At its best, it provides a stockproof barrier, whose shelter can be felt far out into the field.

October 2007

Plate 6
1. Matricaria discoidea DC. –
Pineappleweed
2. Plantago major L. –
Greater Plantain
3. Trifolium repens L. –
White Clover

Initially, I drew everything on transparent greaseproof paper. It was tough enough to withstand a lot of rubbing out. I indicated shadows, textures, veins, etc., and wrote notes on it. As it came on a roll and was the right width, it was versatile and also cheap; a consideration when using large quantities. This worked well until the manufacturers began making it dark brown and opaque. The transparency was crucial as it enabled me to arrange one piece over another and juggle them into the best position.

When I was satisfied with my composition I transferred the image onto the Fabriano using Trace-Down and an automatic pencil H.B. lead 0.5mm thickness. I did not trace down every tiny detail, but referred back to my drawing, keeping the watercolour paper as pristine as possible. The graphite deposited by the sheet of Trace-Down will rub out. Most disappeared during the painting process. I used a kneadable putty rubber, breaking off small pieces to remove any marks still visible. I changed it often and used up the dirty pieces on the drawings.

November 2007

Plate 7
1. **Osmunda regalis** L. – *Royal Fern*
2. **Solanum dulcamara** L. – *Bittersweet*
3. **Blechnum spicant** (L.) Roth – *Hard-fern*

The ferns are not flowering plants, but reproduce by spore, rather than by seed. Their reproductive structures evolved long before flowers and have remained the same for millions of years. So, how could I not paint them, being so ancient, so beautiful and such an integral part of my landscape?

The Royal Fern is very distinctive and can make a huge mound in the right conditions. In this section I showed its lovely autumn colour. The Hard-fern forms a rosette of infertile fronds and the fertile fronds emerge vertically from the centre. I cut the frond part way up and turned it over to show the spores which helps in identification.

Painting the Bittersweet (also known as Woody Nightshade) diagonally across the page helped to indicate its straggling nature.

November 2007

Plate 8
1. **Lolium perenne** L. –
Perennial Rye-grass
2. **Trifolium pratense** L. –
Red Clover
3. **Lolium multiflorum** Lam. –
Italian Rye-grass

Grasses are, of course, flowering plants and have been included in my collection. I have an original 1954 edition of 'Grasses' by C.E. Hubbard which I regard as my grass Bible. As grasses vary in colour greatly, according to their stage of growth and growing conditions, the black and white illustrations by Joan Sampson are no disadvantage.

I quote from inside the jacket: "Grasses are the most abundant, wide spread and useful of all flowering plants".

The Perennial Rye-grass is considered by many to be the most valuable of all the herbage grasses. The improved strains now grown in The British Isles include one called 'Cornish Eaver'. The Red Clover produces a very bulky crop but tends to die out in the older leys. Only a few specimens were found on these old pastures.

December 2007

Gateway to the Cows' Moor

Plate 9
1. Hedera hibernica (G. Kirchn.) Bean –
Irish Ivy
2. Polypodium agg. –
Polypody
3. Ilex aquifolium L. –
Holly

I recorded the month in which each plate was painted. It seemed a bit obvious to group Holly and Ivy together, but the result pleased me. The moss and lichen found near the Polypody balanced the composition although my study did not extend to naming these lower plant forms. The Polypody often grows along the branches of the oak trees. I played safe by calling it Polypodium agg., although it looked most likely to be Polypodium vulgare. Holly berries are often eaten by birds well before Christmas. According to ERICA (Environmental Recording in Cornwall Automated), that is the Cornish Flora database, most Cornish Ivies are named Hedera hibernica.
Reference:- *French C. Erica for Windows (2010)*

While still discovering and recording plants I made endless lists, choosing which to group together. Inevitably the lists suffered frequent alterations. My initial target was to paint one plate per month and complete the whole project within three years. So at first I wasn't putting myself under undue pressure. I could afford to miss a plant here and there. I could leave some until next year, couldn't I?

Alongside this project I continued to paint for the E.P.F.S., The criteria for these botanical paintings is very exacting and they go through a rigorous assessment before being accepted. A Florilegium can be a collection of botanical illustrations at a specific geographical location. For example, The Chelsea Physic Garden, Highgrove House, (home of H.R.H. Prince Charles, Duke of Cornwall,) The Eden Project, and the most extensive and famous of them all, The Royal Botanic Gardens at Kew. Here there are over 200,000 botanical illustrations dating back to about 1760. Compared to Kew, the E.P.F.S. is still in its infancy, but, from little acorns – mighty oak trees grow.

January 2008

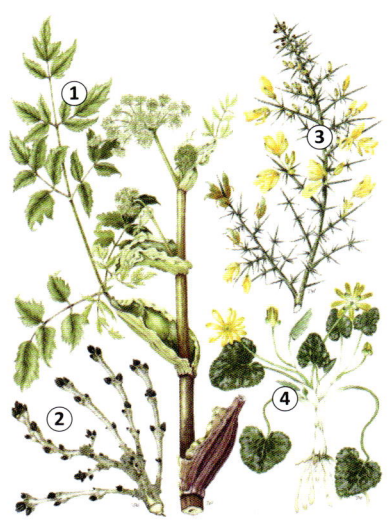

Plate 10
1. **Angelica sylvestris** L. – *Wild Angelica*
2. **Fraxinus excelsior** L. – *Ash*
3. **Ulex europaeus** L. – *Gorse*
4. **Ficaria verna** Schaeff. – *Lesser Celandine*

By choosing to paint Ash buds and bare branches it was possible to keep painting through the winter. The Angelica was an odd one that produced a very late, immature flower head. The inflated sheathing petioles were interesting to paint. Gorse is nearly always flowering, but notice the Celandine. This was the first on my second list of sixty plants, appearing very early, but disappearing completely by July.

As well as the anticipation of discovering new plants as the new year began, my walks were made even more pleasurable by observing other wildlife.

Pheasants and Snipe are often startled out of the rushes. Wrens and Goldcrests work along the hedges. Frogspawn is abundant. Some, in the waterlogged wheel ruts of tractors, is doomed to die. Otherwise, it is confined to the more sluggish ditches and the pond, rather than the faster-flowing water. Moorhens and Mallards frequent the pond and the Heron is an occasional visitor.

February and April 2008

Plate 11
1. **Salix cinerea** L. – *Grey Willow*
2. **Oxalis acetosella** L. – *Wood-sorrel*
3. **Asplenium scolopendrium** L. – *Hart's-tongue*

I couldn't resist the fallen willow branch, clothed in moss and bracket fungus. While these last two were not part of my study, they, along with the decaying branch, describe so well the ancient hedgerows and the Common which borders the South side of the moor.

The Common is heavily wooded, extremely wet, dark and impenetrable. From time to time foxes breed there. Once, I saw two cubs playing well out into the Bullocks' Moor. They took no notice of me walking slowly among the cattle. One day, after seeing them regularly, I took my camera. I got my snapshot, but the click of the shutter was heard and sent them speeding back to the cover of the trees.

The Wood-sorrel is quite scarce and, strangely, occurs only in two small patches at opposite ends of the moor, clinging on just above the water line.

February 2008

Plate 12
1. **Poa annua** L. – *Annual Meadow-grass*
2. **Veronica hederifolia** L. – *Ivy-leaved Speedwell*
3. **Cardamine flexuosa** With. – *Wavy Bitter-cress*
4. **Taraxacum** agg. – Dandelion

I used Winsor and Newton Series 7 miniature sable brushes sizes 1, 2 and 3 throughout. They were good for the small flowers such as the Speedwells and Grasses and when loaded with paint coped well with the larger leaves. A hand lens x10 magnification was an essential tool in identification. I also worked through a clip-on magnifier which kept both hands free, one for holding the brush, the other for holding a folded tissue ready to lift or blot. I protected the surrounding area with tissues. I referred back to my drawing for details and often kept a small piece of plant material under the magnifier.

The Dandelion has been entered as an un-named member of the genus Taraxacum. About eighty species have been recorded for Cornwall. Most of the entries in this book follow Stace's Flora (3rd Edition).

Stace, C.A. *New Flora of the British Isles*, Third Edition.
Cambridge: Cambridge University Press 2010
ISBN 978-0-521-70772-5

March 2008

Plate 13
1. **Glechoma hederacea** L. – *Ground-ivy*
2. **Veronica persica** Poir. – *Common Field-speedwell*
3. **Luzula campestris** (L.) DC. – *Field wood-rush*
4. **Veronica filiformis** Sm. – *Slender Speedwell*
5. **Potentilla sterilis** (L.) Garcke – *Barren Strawberry*

There is a south-facing grassy bank bordering the farm lane and separated from the moor by the road. I planted it up with species Crocuses, Snowdrops, Grape Hyacinths and Cyclamineous Hybrid Narcissi such as February Gold, Jet Fire and Jack Snipe and that little gem Tête à Tête. The Tenby Daffodil, Narcissus obvallaris also found a place. I never cut the grass until after 'Royal Cornwall'.

Without further attention from me this bank has gradually turned itself into a wildflower meadow. The list of its residents would make a florilegium by itself. Celandine, Primrose, Barren Strawberry, Field Woodrush, Common Sorrel, Dandelion, Speedwell, Cuckooflower, Ribwort Plantain, Sweet Vernal and others smother it in the Spring.

All these wild flowers also inhabit nooks and crannies, open spaces and shady hollows in the moor.

March and April 2008

Plate 14
1. **Narcissus** agg. – *Daffodil*
2. **Viola riviniana** Rchb. – *Common Dog-violet*
3. **Allium triquetrum** L. – *Three-cornered Garlic*

The impact of this Spring-like composition was heightened by the combination of warm and cool colours. This was not unlike a wild daffodil - Narcissus pseudonarcissus - in form and colour, but was more likely to be a garden escape. I recorded and painted everything, whether native or naturalized. For example, the Slender Speedwell on Plate 13 was introduced from the Caucasus.

The daffodils were found on a tiny island formed when the watercourse had divided and rejoined itself at the lower end of Menna Moor abutting the Common. They were safe from the trampling of cattle, behind the electric fence. I imagined their bulbs being borne downstream with some garden waste and washing up on the island.

Roe Deer as well as foxes use the cover of the Common. One, startled by my presence, sprang away but was checked, momentarily, by the electric fence wire, giving me a few more seconds to observe it.

March and June 2008

Plate 15
1. **Lythrum portula** (L.) D.A. Webb – *Water-purslane*
2. **Ranunculus omiophyllus** Ten. – *Round-leaved Crowfoot*
3. **Cochlearia officinalis** L. – *Common Scurvy-grass*
4. **Sibthorpia europaea** L. – *Cornish Moneywort*
5. **Callitriche stagnalis** Scop. – *Common Water-Starwort*
6. **Chrysosplenium oppositifolium** L. – *Opposite-leaved Golden-saxifrage*

This plate of small water lovers was done in March although I had to wait until June for the Water Purslane. What had been plentiful the previous year was not so evident in 2008 as it was much drier.

Francis Rose's 'Wild Flower Key' was one of the books I found most useful. In it the Cornish Moneywort is listed as an ancient woodland indicator plant in the South West. It seems to thrive around the deep water-retaining holes left by the cattle's feet. The flowers were added at a later date after growing a piece on in a seed tray. I also grew the Golden Saxifrage in a seed tray until it flowered. I then replanted them both. As we are owner-occupiers of the land I did not have to seek permission to pick specimens. I was, though, always mindful that wild plants should not be disturbed wantonly.

A spring rises out in Menna Moor and finds its way to the edge of the field by way of an open drainage ditch. In March, the Round-leaved Crowfoot formed a bright green sward, studded with tiny white flowers. Upon turn-out the cows churned the area into a black soup. It was not long before the water had formed a clear channel again and the crowfoot was back. It can be found anywhere across the field in water-retaining pockets.

April 2008

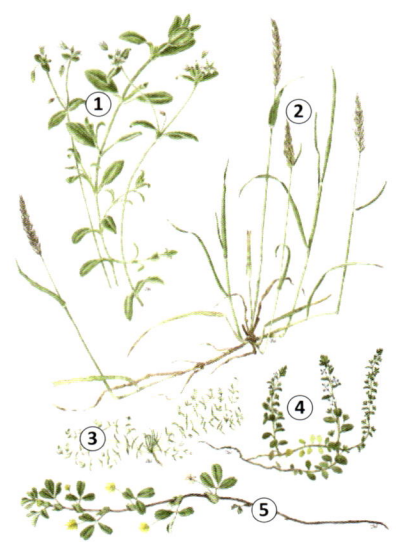

Plate 16
1. **Cerastium fontanum** Baumg. – *Common Mouse-ear*
2. **Anthoxanthum odoratum** L. – *Sweet Vernal-grass*
3. **Sagina procumbens** L. – *Procumbent Pearlwort*
4. **Veronica serpyllifolia** L. – *Thyme-leaved Speedwell*
5. **Trifolium dubium** Sibth. – *Lesser Trefoil*

The Sweet Vernal grass, being one of the earliest to flower, is a welcome sight. It was, at one time, included in seed mixtures for hay and pasture on account of its fragrance, but has a high proportion of stem to leaf, making it less valuable than for instance the ryegrasses.

Seeing the Sweet Vernal everywhere, somehow reminded me of the grassy Wiltshire plain. I have stood accused, more than once, of habitually keeping my eyes on the ground. If not for that, I would have missed the hare, that day, in the Cows' Moor. It was crouched, ears flattened, at the foot of the hedge. We stared at each other and for a moment, time stood still. Then it bolted into the rushes. My first sighting of a hare, since my days growing up in Wiltshire, made it a day to remember.

Every plant presents a new challenge to the artist. The Common Mouse-ear, having very hairy leaves and stems, is no exception. In order to best show the structure of the Procumbent Pearlwort, I unravelled it a bit. The whole plant forms a matted cushion and is common on paths, lawns and flower beds. During this Spring period, I was able to complete the Speedwells which totalled seven.

May 2008

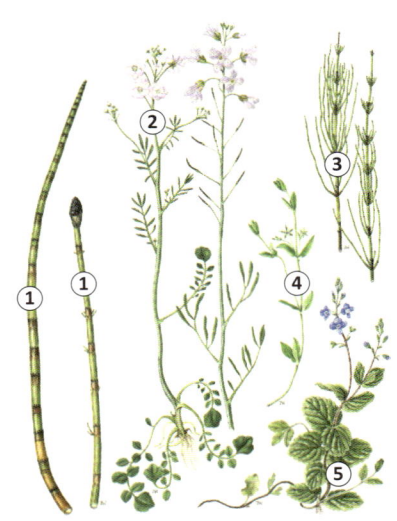

Plate 17
1. *Equisetum fluviatile* L. –
Water Horsetail
2. *Cardamine pratensis* L. –
Cuckooflower
3. *Equisetum palustre* L. –
Marsh Horsetail
4. *Stellaria alsine* Grimm –
Bog Stitchwort
5. *Veronica chamaedrys* L. –
Germander Speedwell

I relied on fresh plant material throughout, which meant constant vigilance and much walking to catch things at the right stage. The initial recording of the species was only the start. Frequent visits to the fields were necessary. Sometimes I made a bee-line to a specific plant. At other times, that is, two or three times a week, I just roamed, looking and making more lists.

For example, I was poised to paint the Water Horsetail, when a sharp frost wiped them out. I waited for more to emerge. When I found one with a cone, the phrase 'bird in the hand' came to me. I rushed home to paint it, only to find plenty at a later date. The Marsh Horsetail was less common and I found none with a cone.

The Cuckooflower (also known as Lady's Smock) comes in the double and single forms and quite a variation in colour. With these petals, I applied a fairly wet, fairly strong colour, then blotted with tissue before it dried. This took out most of the pigment, but kept the light, so important in watercolour painting. I added the veins and shading last.

May 2008

Plate 18
1. Hyacinthoides non-scripta (L.) Chouard ex Rothm. – *Bluebell*
2. Stellaria holostea L. – *Greater Stitchwort*
3. Silene dioica (L.) Clairv. – *Red Campion*

These three seemed obvious companions. The Red Campion is dioecious. This means it has only male flowers on some plants and only female flowers on others. This one is a male specimen. The female flower would have an inflated seed capsule with strongly re-curved capsule teeth.

I didn't allow myself to indulge, much, in idle speculation about the future of this florilegium. With this group, however, for a brief moment, I thought they might work as a print with three separate windows in the mount.

With the Greater Stitchwort, I encountered the problem of painting white flowers on white paper. By choosing not to overlap the different plants, I didn't give myself the option of putting a green leaf behind a white flower; a technique used so successfully by W. Keble Martin.

May 2008

Plate 19
1. **Myosotis secunda** Al. Murray – *Creeping Forget-me-not*
2. **Ranunculus repens** L. – *Creeping Buttercup*
3. **Silene flos-cuculi** (L.) Clairv. – *Ragged-Robin*
4. **Veronica montana** L. – *Wood Speedwell*
5. **Galium palustre** L. – *Common Marsh-bedstraw*

Where possible, I showed the cross section through the stem. It helped to convey the form and showed whether the stem was solid, hollow, round, square, ridged or hairy; all aspects which aid identification. I flooded the area with strong pigment. After a moment, I dropped in a blob of clean water. This shoots the pigment out to the edge. After a further moment, I lifted the water out of the centre with the point of a tissue. If it went according to plan, it left a thin hard line around the edge. With a hollow stem, I repeated the process and added a shadow on one side of the hollow.

It occurred to me then, that at its simplest, watercolour painting is just a combination of hard edges and soft edges. A hard edge, as I have just described, and a soft edge, where the pigment is allowed to bleed into damp paper.

May 2008

The farm lies close to the China Clay Works.

The clay burrows have been encouraged to grow vegetation, which in turn encourages buzzards. As many as ten together have been observed while ploughing the arable ground. Often in the moor, they can be seen wheeling high overhead.

The Tufted Hair-grass was new to me. I showed three lengths of stem which fitted together. By drawing it on the roll of greaseproof paper and then cutting it into sections, I knew the ends would match. Where appropriate, I showed the back and front aspect of flowers.

Another plant, previously unknown to me, was the Three-nerved Sandwort. Sometimes it is the little things that have the 'wow' factor. It first came to my notice on a wild flower walk, guided by Keith Spurgin. He took members of the E.P.F.S. to the Luxulyan Valley and Treffry Viaduct. To come upon an unfamiliar plant and have it instantly and correctly identified was a real bonus. Were it not for that, I might still be dismissing it as Common Chickweed. During that walk, on May 4th 2008, I recorded in excess of 120 plants.

Plate 20
1. **Deschampsia cespitosa** (L.) P. Beauv. – *Tufted Hair-grass*
2. **Geum urbanum** L. – *Wood Avens*
3. **Moehringia trinervia** (L.) Clairv. – *Three-nerved Sandwort*
4. **Potentilla anserina** L. – *Silverweed*

I was surprised to find I had completed four plates in May.

Was it possible to complete the project in two years?

June 2008

September 1980

May 1982

Plate 21
1. **Dactylis glomerata** L. – *Cock's-foot*
2. **Ajuga reptans** L. – *Bugle*
3. **Leucanthemum vulgare** Lam. – *Oxeye Daisy*
4. **Cynosurus cristatus** L. – *Crested Dog's-tail*
5. **Holcus lanatus** L. – *Yorkshire-fog*

I found only this one Bugle spike, and was loth to pick it. As it spreads by means of runners I hoped it would continue to grow. With just one spike I had to get a move-on. I did all my painting on the kitchen table. The windows face North and East giving good light. It was always warm and I didn't have to pack it away every day.

Quite early on I had to devise a method which was sustainable, alongside the inevitable domestic distractions. The kitchen is the hub of a farm and, although we are officially retired and occupying a small converted barn, some things never change. John and I still sit down to a hot meal at midday and he still shares in the farm work every day. So, in the kitchen I can cook and continue to think and plan (in fact there is always more thinking time involved than actual brush work). Farm traffic passes the window, so I keep in touch. If I had to disappear into a remote studio, I doubt if this florilegium would ever have been completed.

June 2008

If it were not for the grazing animals, the moor would soon revert to scrubland.

There are two 'wow' moments on this plate. The Yellow Bartsia was one of only two growing where a spring rises in Robin's Meadow. I dug it up, keeping the root ball intact. I kept it in a bucket of water and re-planted it as quickly as possible. It re-appeared in 2009. The other 'wow' is the Bog Pimpernel, of which I found one patch the size of a dinner plate. An electric fence surrounds Menna Moor to keep the cows in. The Bog Pimpernel was located directly below the wire. In past years, I have regularly pared back the brambles and rushes along the wire but never before noticed this little gem.

The Soft-rush is, by far, the most dominant, although several smaller rushes and sedges find a home. Controlling the soft rush by topping is proving to be a losing battle. As the ground becomes boggier, less can be reached without the tractor getting stuck. Even willows have taken hold in places. If it were not for the grazing animals, it would soon revert to scrubland, and smaller, less aggressive species would be crowded out.

Plate 22
1. **Juncus articulatus** L. – *Jointed Rush*
2. **Carex leporina** L. – *Oval Sedge*
3. **Isolepis setacea** (L.) R. Br. – *Bristle Club-rush*
4. **Anagallis tenella** (L.) L. – *Bog Pimpernel*
5. **Luzula multiflora** (Ehrh.) Lej. – *Heath Wood-rush*
6. **Parentucellia viscosa** (L.) Caruel – *Yellow Bartsia*
7. **Juncus effusus** L. – *Soft-rush*
8. **Juncus bufonius** L. – *Toad Rush*

Willows encroaching into the moor.

July 2008

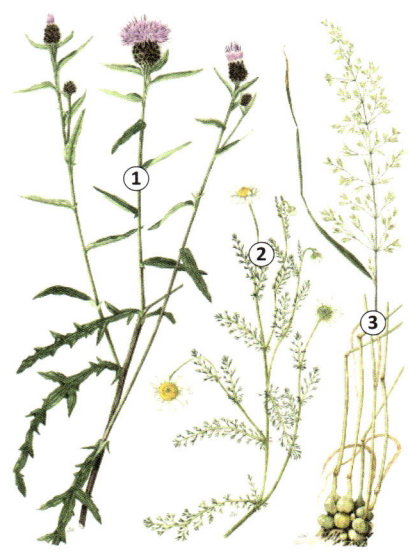

Plate 23
1. Centaurea nigra L. –
Common Knapweed
2. Anthemis arvensis L. –
Corn Chamomile
3. Arrhenatherum elatius (L.) P. Beauv. Ex J. & C. Presl –
False Oat-grass

These three were also found in Robin's Meadow, a small triangular paddock, grazed only occasionally by a pony. Here, the knapweed reaches giant proportions. At this time, I also painted the Common Knapweed for the Eden Archive. Magnificent as are the biomes at The Eden Project, there are other areas of great interest to me. One is 'Wild Cornwall'. The painting members of E.P.F.S. have taken on the task of painting all the species found in that area. On one visit in mid-September 2009 I found evidence of well over 100 species.

For variety and to aid identification, I often included roots and bulbs. This False Oat-grass (also known as Onion Couch) was so congested, the bulbs were quite exposed, giving them a greenish tinge. As it was at least five feet tall, I painted just the head and the bulbs.

The Corn Chamomile is an endangered Red Data Species (2005). I would like to think I have identified it correctly. Upon examination under the hand lens, my specimen had many of the features attributed to Corn Chamomile, for example:- receptacle in cross-section was solid, there was a style at the base of each ray floret and each disc floret had a transparent scale.

Two aspects of a Sycamore Tree:- Left, wind revealing grey/green underside of the leaves. Below, strange root formations protruding from the hedge.

July 2008

Plate 24
1. Senecio vulgaris L. –
Groundsel
2. Gnaphalium uliginosum L.
Marsh Cudweed
3. Lamium purpureum L. –
Red Dead-nettle
4. Lepidium didymus L. –
Lesser Swine-cress
5. Hypericum humifusum L. –
Trailing St John's-wort
6. Polygonum aviculare L. –
Knotgrass

Following the hard winter of 2009/2010 the blossom was brilliant. Hawthorn and Elder were particularly noticeable.

There comes a stage in every painting where I feel it is going badly. I begin to doubt my abilities. Plate 24 was a struggle for some reason. I have learnt to recognise the symptoms. I found the best answer was to keep on and work through it. There is a saying that those who never make a mistake, never make anything. It is also said that if a job is worth doing it is worth doing well. I believe the reverse to be true also, if a job is worth doing it is worth doing badly. Far better to do it badly than not try at all.

These subjects on Plate 24 tend to grow where earth has been recently disturbed, in trodden gateways, areas around cattle feeders and road verges.

August 2008

Plate 25
1. **Calluna vulgaris** (L.) Hull – *Heather*
2. **Teucrium scorodonia** L. – *Wood Sage*
3. **Erica cinerea** L. – *Bell Heather*

South-facing aspect.

I like to paint much wetter than some botanical artists. I often finished a leaf with a transparent glaze. When the underlying detail was completely dry, I washed clear water over the light areas and a darker wash in the shadows. I kept on until the paper was glistening. The Fabriano tolerated this treatment and as long as I didn't scrub, the underlying detail was undisturbed. Some of the tiny leaves and flowers were very time consuming. It was worth persevering to get the effect of the whole spray. In some cases it became as repetitive as cross-stitch and strangely calming. At other times I lost patience and found it best to walk away and return to it later.

These three subjects grew in a similar habitat, along the top and sides of a dry hedge, among the roots of gnarled oak trees. In the ditches below, grew water-loving subjects, such as figwort and crowfoot. What odd combinations growing within a few feet of each other!

North-facing aspect.

August 2008

Plate 26
1. Corylus avellana L. – *Hazel*
2. Fagus sylvatica L. – *Beech*
3. Acer pseudoplatanus L. – *Sycamore*
4. Sambucus nigra L. – *Elder*
5. Betula pubescens Ehrh. – *Downy Birch*

With this study of trees I completed all the trees on the list except for the Cornish Elm. Betula pubescens, liking wetter ground, is more common in the area than Betula pendula. There is a hybrid between the two but this has not been recorded for Cornwall. The total number of trees was twelve. As I approached the half-way mark being able to tick off a plant, a whole plate or a group of plants helped to keep me focussed. I have never minded working alone and never turn on the radio. Sometimes urgent gardening jobs intruded, such as harvesting peas.

I cultivate a vegetable garden, fashioned out of waste ground behind the buildings. It has become very productive and keeps the two of us supplied with fresh vegetables and soft fruit for much of the year. I freeze any surplus for use over the winter. When the peas are ready they take priority. I want them at their best and they will not wait.

Another area of the Eden Project I find fascinating is the allotment. It was from this allotment that I sourced the Sweet Potato – Ipomaea batatus. One painting went into the Eden Archive, the other won for me the supply of miniature brushes.

August 2008

Plate 27
1. *Stachys sylvatica* L. – *Hedge Woundwort*
2. *Galium aparine* L. – *Cleavers*
3. *Galeopsis tetrahit* L. – *Common Hemp-nettle*
4. *Heracleum sphondylium* L. – *Hogweed*
5. *Arum maculatum* L. – *Lords-and-Ladies*

For a change I chose to paint some seed heads. August 2008 was wet and miserable. The harvest was a disaster. The oats, for instance, looked alright from a distance, but on closer inspection, was little more than empty husks. The repercussions of a bad harvest are felt for a long time afterwards. Harvesting and drying costs are greater than in a good harvest and the animals still have to eat the poor grain.

Once, when we were still totally reliant on hay for winter fodder and making about 8000 bales annually, 10 acres was ruined. During the three weeks after mowing the grass it rained just often enough to prevent baling. It had to be removed from the field as the grass underneath was suffering and we needed the field to recover for further grazing. So we dumped it all. Nowadays with silage made by foragers and round balers it is much easier and little is wasted.

So back to 2008, and it was hard to find even a Hogweed that wasn't bedraggled. However, the Cuckoo Pint still managed to shine. There are other local names for Arum maculatum. This is the one I grew up using and things learnt early in life tend to stick.

August 2008

Cows and calves in the 'Undertown' around the old wheelpit.

Plate 28
1. Pulicaria dysenterica (L.) Bernh. – *Common Fleabane*
2. Lycopus europaeus L. – *Gypsywort*
3. Carex demissa Hornem. – *Common Yellow-sedge*

I always looked for colour in leaves other than green, and yes, the Gypsywort leaves really were this colour. When I first found it in a wet area of the Cows' Moor I had no idea what it was and couldn't recall ever seeing it in any book. I found it hard to believe I had missed so many things in fifty years. My excuse was that I had been studying the livestock more. This also required constant vigilance. One of my worst moments came when I found two calves dead one morning. It turned out to be a Salmonella infection which we traced to someone's load of pig manure spilling on the road and polluting the streams. The same streams where I had paddled and built dams with my children and later on my grandchildren.

All sick animals found their way into my care. I studied for a National Certificate in Agriculture at Moulton Farm Institute, Northamptonshire, and won, I suspect by default, a copy of Black's Veterinary Dictionary 1953 edition. By virtue of this, I was deemed by the family to be the expert in all things veterinary. The loss of an animal was always keenly felt and more so if it could have been avoided.

September 2008

Plate 29
1. Crepis capillaris (L.) Wallr. –
Smooth Hawk's-beard
2. Stellaria media (L.) Vill. –
Common Chickweed
3. Lapsana communis L. –
Nipplewort

From the yard, a sunken lane drops towards the granite horse trough, filled from the overflowing pond.

Sometimes pictures speak louder than words and the delicate tracery of the combined seed heads and flowers here are a reminder that even the commonest plant has its own unique beauty and character. This is what I have tried to portray. The leaves at the base give the composition some weight.

At one time, the water from the pond was channelled across the Undertown (meaning the field below the farmstead) to work a water wheel. This wheel was removed during the war to help the war effort.

The water now runs on down the lane, rejoining the streams at the lower corner of the Bullocks' Moor. This lane is rich in Brooklime and Waterpepper.

September 2008

Plate 30
1. **Tamus communis** L. – *Black Bryony*
2. **Pteridium aquilinum** (L.) Kuhn – *Bracken*
3. **Galium album** Mill. – *Hedge Bedstraw*

I had been looking forward to this plate and could picture in my mind the combination of Bracken and Black Bryony as it twines on the hedges. This is the only time two plants have overlapped. The berries looked even more dramatic after I had taken the advice of my tutor, Mally, and deepened the shadows to give more contrast. As she often tells her students : "Dare to be dark!".

I have said before that I like to paint 'wet-in-wet', after all it is water colour. I indulged myself on the Black Bryony leaves and had fun dropping in the different colours. I opted to paint the seeds of the Hedge Bedstraw. I am sure they were only marginally less difficult than the flowers would have been.

October 2008

Plate 31
1. **Digitalis purpurea** L. – *Foxglove*
2. **Achillea millefolium** L. – *Yarrow*
3. **Stellaria graminea** L. – *Lesser Stitchwort*

In October 2008, Foxglove flowers were hard to find, unlike the previous autumn when they went on very late. It was probably due to the generally poor autumn weather. Normally, many plants will produce second growth in the autumn, but nothing is certain. If I were to embark on another field study at some time in the future, would I find more or fewer species or even some new ones? I had hoped to find at least one orchid as they were present some years ago. Here again, I combined a Foxglove seed head with a flowering stem.

The Yarrow leaf was another of those fiddly jobs which can drive one mad. The Lesser Stitchwort, as well as being daintier, can be distinguished from the Greater Stitchwort by flowering somewhat later.

October 2008

Plate 32
1. Asplenium adiantum-nigrum
L. – *Black Spleenwort*
2. Umbilicus rupestris (Salisb.) Dandy –
Navelwort
3. Asplenium trichomanes L. –
Maidenhair Spleenwort

I often included a dead or dying leaf, as I liked the colour contrasts and it indicated Nature's continual cycle of growth and decay.

It's always interesting to speculate on how a plant arrived at its location. The road to the North of Menna Moor is several feet higher than the field and a length of retaining wall was built. I suspect that the loads of stone brought to the site may have harboured this solitary Maidenhair Spleenwort. The Navelwort and Black Spleenwort are both widespread.

November 2008 and April 2009

Plate 33
1. Sonchus asper (L.) Hill –
Prickly Sowthistle
2. Cirsium vulgare (Savi) Ten. –
Spear Thistle
3. Fumaria muralis Sond. ex W.D.J. Koch Ssp. boraei (Jord.) Pugsley –
Common Ramping-fumitory
4. Geranium dissectum L. –
Cut-leaved Crane's-bill

At the end of 2008, plant material became scarce. Some of those which were available had already been painted the previous year which had to be good news. I had to wait until April to complete the Common Ramping-fumitory and Cut-leaved Crane's-bill. The latter made a rosette of leaves over winter. The flowering stems, when they emerged, were so dense with leaves that I concentrated on the flowers, just indicating where a leaf or stalk began.

There are two weeds which we try to control on the farm. The Spear Thistles, if allowed to spread, make huge plants, avoided by sheep and cattle, thus reducing the grazing area. The other one we do not tolerate is the Common Ragwort. Pulling ragwort was one of my regular tasks which is why you won't see one in my collection. We have no quarrel with the Marsh Ragwort which provides food for the Cinnabar moth caterpillars. I have often seen these black and orange striped caterpillars, but never on the Common Ragwort.

Pond and farmhouse January 1969 & May 2010.

January 2009

Plate 34
1. Polystichum setiferum (Forssk.) T. Moore ex Woyn –
Soft Shield-fern
2. Viola odorata L. –
Sweet Violet
3. Vinca minor L. –
Lesser Periwinkle

At the beginning of 2009, I wrote a list of the remaining plants with provisional groupings. This Soft Shield-fern remained evergreen and retained its spores long enough to paint in January. At the highest North-East corner is a well, used by local people in days gone by. When I found these three around the well, a torrent of water was gushing out of it. I assumed the violet was a garden escape as this is the only location other than a verge opposite a nearby cottage. The well area is also closely carpeted by Ramsons.

March 2009

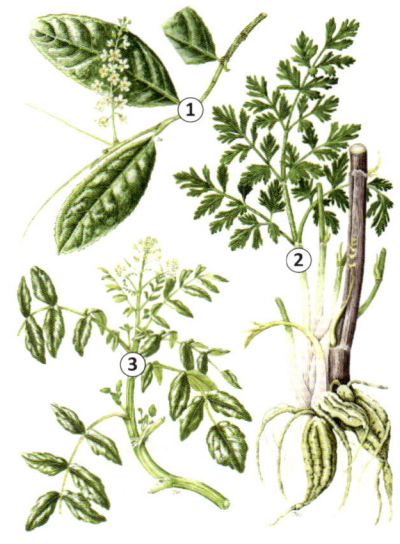

Plate 35
1. **Prunus laurocerasus** L. – *Cherry Laurel*
2. **Oenanthe crocata** L. – *Hemlock Water-dropwort*
3. **Nasturtium officinale** W.T. Aiton – *Water-cress*

This Laurel was encroaching from a garden, again near the well. I combined it with the water-cress and the Hemlock Water-dropwort simply because I was running out of choices. One more indication that progress was being made.

This is real water-cress as opposed to Fool's water-cress. Still, nothing is simple. The book lists two depending on whether the seed pods have two rows or one. No real problem, I thought, until I found the cows had eaten it all before it set seed.

Cows eating everything, reminded me that some years ago, a neighbour dug out his ditches and threw everything back onto the field, exposing the roots of the Hemlock Water-dropwort. Within a few hours he had lost more than a dozen cows. According to my copy of Black's the symptoms appear very quickly and death follows in one to four hours. The mucous membranes become congested and the victim expires in violent convulsions! Having said all that, I know our cows sometimes eat the young leaves without ill-effect. We don't go out of our way to get rid of the plants, although I did burn the roots of the one I painted.

March 2009

Plate 36
1. Oxalis articulata Savigny –
Pink-sorrel
2. Allium ursinum L. –
Ramsons
3. Primula x polyantha Mill. –
Polyanthus
4. Primula vulgaris Huds. –
Primrose

Wild Primroses were very scarce, but a few multi-headed types were evident. They were probably garden escapes, as is the Pink Sorrel. I just showed one head of Wild Primrose to compare it with the much larger and deeper yellow specimens.

Spring blooms can be enjoyed while the trees above are still leafless.

April 2009

Through the winter and early spring I had been keeping pace with plant growth. Suddenly that was no longer the case. April brought an explosion of new growth and panic began to set in. I was determined to finish in 2009 and not to miss anything that would have meant waiting another year. Painting from photographs or someone else's work was not an option. There was no choice but to raise my game.

Plate 37
1. **Plantago lanceolata** L. – *Ribwort Plantain*
2. **Cerastium glomeratum** Thuill. – *Sticky Mouse-ear*
3. **Rumex acetosa** L. – *Common Sorrel*
4. **Bellis perennis** L. – *Daisy*
5. **Taraxacum** – Little Marsh-dandelion

W. Keble Martin lists a similar dandelion as Little Marsh-dandelion. It is widespread throughout the moor but comes and goes very quickly in late April. In 2008, at the very end of its season, I realised it was different from other dandelions. It was too late to paint it then but in 2009 I was waiting for it. Francis Rose groups all the many dandelions together. The bracts on this one remain adpressed to the head. Taraxacum nordstedtii Dahlst has bracts much like this, variable leaves and has been recorded fairly frequently (for a dandelion) in Cornwall, and within less than 10km of Menna.

Below:- Little Marsh-dandelion clocks and Sweet Vernal-grass in the Cows' Moor.

April 2009

Plate 38
1. Alliaria petiolata (M. Bieb.) Cavara & Grande – *Garlic Mustard*
2. Geranium robertianum L. – *Herb-Robert*
3. Poa trivialis L. – *Rough Meadow-grass*

From here on, this project took over my life. When my total reached 200, John said "You can't stop there, people will think you are cheating". There was no chance of that, as with several grasses emerging, my total soon mounted to 209.

The paintings were the first thing I saw in the morning. The window sills were full of plant material in various stages of decay. If I wasn't painting, I was thinking about painting, making more lists or rushing out for fresh leaves. It wasn't enough to finish one plate before beginning the next. Now, two or three were in progress simultaneously.

Throughout this state of turmoil John was always supportive, never complained and entered into the spirit of the enterprise by bringing in plants for me to identify.

April 2009

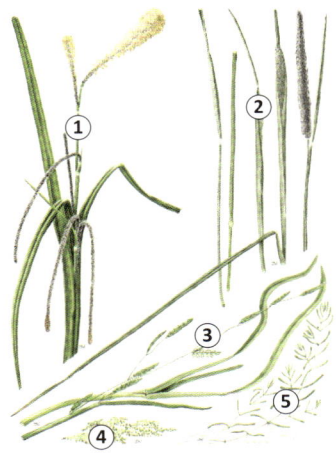

Plate 39
1. **Carex pendula** Huds. – *Pendulous Sedge*
2. **Alopecurus pratensis** L. – *Meadow Foxtail*
3. **Glyceria fluitans** (L.) R. Br. – *Floating Sweet-grass*
4. **Lemna minor** L. – *Common Duckweed*
5. **Callitriche brutia** Petagna –
Intermediate (or Pedunculate) *Water-starwort*

Floating Sweet-grass, which clogs the ditches in April, is another plant which the cows enjoy when they first go out after a winter on silage. I was pleased to catch the Pendulous Sedge when the male flower was at its fluffiest, as it soon becomes brown and drab. It can be difficult, in a small space, to convey the form of what can be a very large plant.

Mixed in with the tiny Lemna minor was the even smaller Lemna minuta. Kunth. (first recognised in the British Isles in 1977). The two often completely cover the surface of the pond.

At this time in my search for new plants, I realised I also had to look under water. The overflow from the pond runs into a large stone drinking trough. I found it to be full of the Intermediate Water-starwort. The two subspecies of Callitriche brutia (ssp brutia and ssp hamulata) are easy to confuse.

May 2009

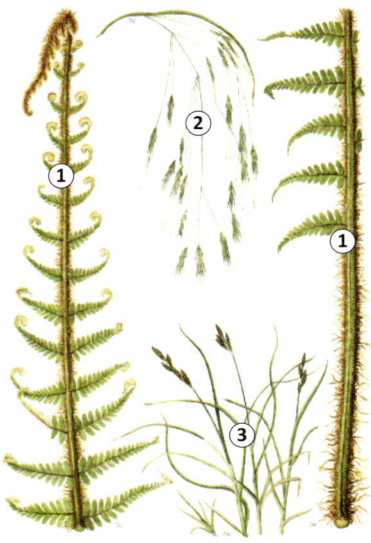

Plate 40
1. Dryopteris affinis agg. –
Golden-scaled Male-fern (group)
2. Anisantha sterilis (L.) Nevski –
Barren Brome
3. Carex leporina L. –
Oval Sedge (immature stage)

This fern looked quite spectacular. By this stage, I knew I had to get to grips with the remaining ferns and was waiting for them to emerge. As soon as I brought the frond into the warmth of the kitchen, it began to uncurl. I did the drawing as fast as possible and my roll of transparent paper then came into its own. I drew the whole frond and separated it on the page. I have indicated where the pinnules begin in the right hand piece. If I had painted them in their entirety, there would have been insufficient room to add a second and third plant. At this stage of growth, no spores were evident, but the brilliant scales were irresistible.

I had doubts about the small sedge and what I first identified as Carex caryophyllea may well be an immature Carex leporina – see also plate 22.

May 2009

Plate 41
1. Dryopteris dilatata (Hoffm.) A. Gray – *Broad Buckler-fern*
2. Dryopteris filix-mas (L.) Schott – *Male-fern*
3. Athyrium filix-femina (L.) Roth – *Lady-fern*

These three ferns brought the total of the ferns up to twelve. Thanks to the Fern Guide I was able to shed some light on what had been a very confusing subject.

Broad Buckler-fern has scales with a dark stripe and is tri-pinnate. Lady-fern has a wine coloured stipe and rachis and is bi-pinnate. Male-fern is also bi-pinnate.

The Fern Guide also covers Horsetails, of which I found two, illustrated on Plate 17. The Water Horsetail was found at the lowest point of all in the Cows' Moor. When first negotiating this swampy area I was forced to climb down into the main river and walk upstream on the firm gravel bed until I had passed the swamp. Even in the driest periods, I have never been confident of crossing it on foot and the Horsetails I painted were picked around its margins. The book touches on alien fern species which are grown commercially as house plants. One such is Cyrtomium falcatum which I discovered growing in the barn on a damp wall. I potted it up and kept it indoors until it grew too big, now it survives in the garden.

May 2009

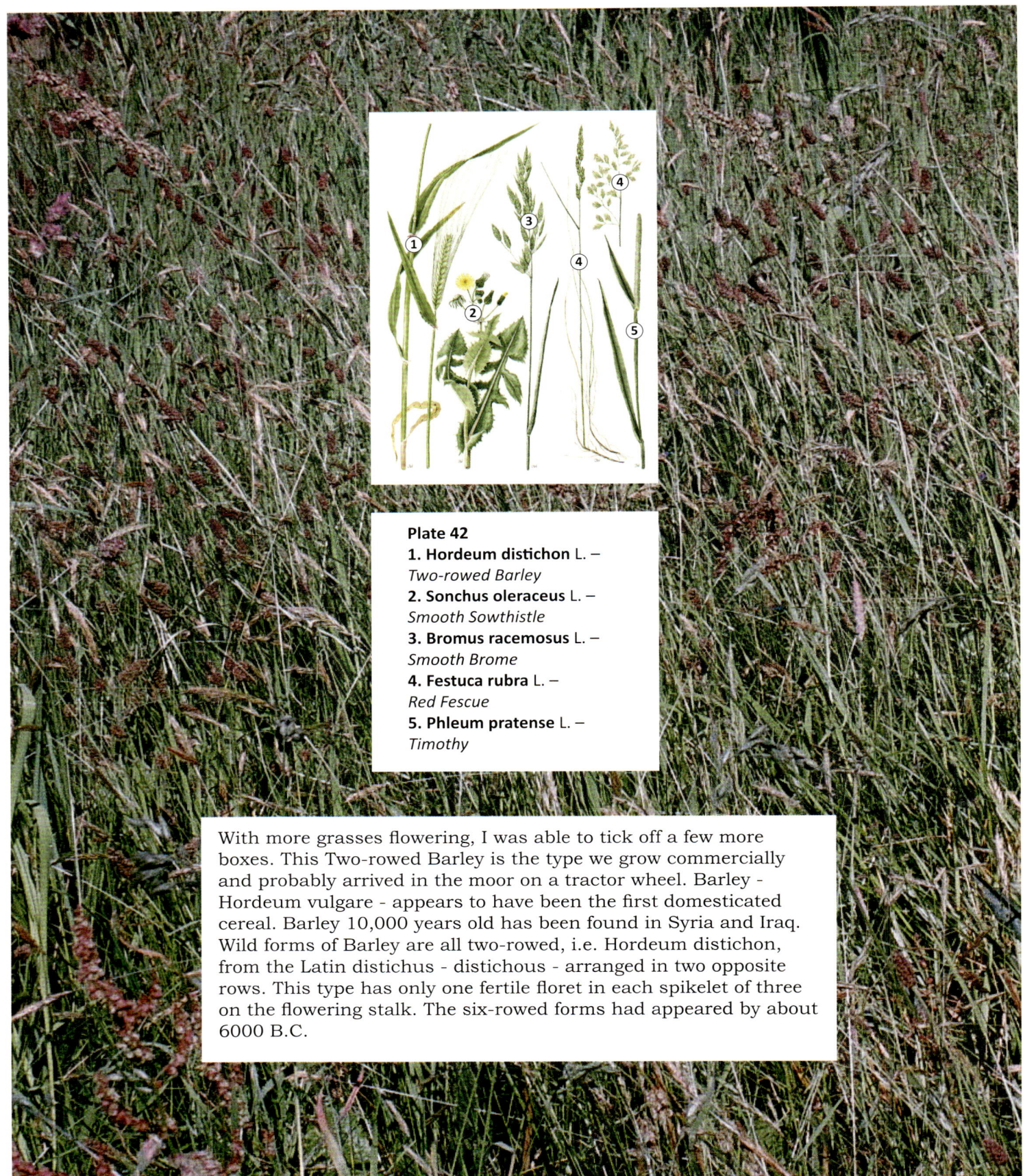

Plate 42
1. **Hordeum distichon** L. –
Two-rowed Barley
2. **Sonchus oleraceus** L. –
Smooth Sowthistle
3. **Bromus racemosus** L. –
Smooth Brome
4. **Festuca rubra** L. –
Red Fescue
5. **Phleum pratense** L. –
Timothy

With more grasses flowering, I was able to tick off a few more boxes. This Two-rowed Barley is the type we grow commercially and probably arrived in the moor on a tractor wheel. Barley - Hordeum vulgare - appears to have been the first domesticated cereal. Barley 10,000 years old has been found in Syria and Iraq. Wild forms of Barley are all two-rowed, i.e. Hordeum distichon, from the Latin distichus - distichous - arranged in two opposite rows. This type has only one fertile floret in each spikelet of three on the flowering stalk. The six-rowed forms had appeared by about 6000 B.C.

May 2009

This combination of vetches had been planned long before and was one of the few to remain unchanged. I was pleased with the effect of the flowers and seed pods. I found the Common Vetch to be very variable. It had from one to four flowers in a leaf axil, some stalked, some not. Some stipules had a dark spot, some did not. Some tendrils were simple, some branched. All the flowers were bright pink, but the reverse of some was pale mauve. All the pods were hairless and dark purple/black. W. Keble Martin lists one - Vicia Angustifolia - where the pods spread and burst the calyx, which mine did.

I painted two small umbels of the Cow Parsley. One showing the flowers, one the seeds. At the time, the foliage was, for me, a leaf too far.

Plate 43
1. Lathyrus pratensis L. –
Meadow Vetchling
2. Vicia cracca L. –
Tufted Vetch
3. Anthriscus sylvestris (L.) Hoffm. –
Cow Parsley
4. Vicia sativa L. –
Common Vetch

June 2009

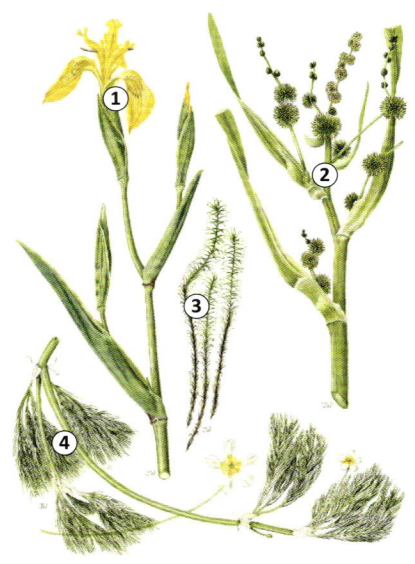

Here are two near disasters. I had earmarked a good clump of Iris the previous autumn, but wanted to wait and paint a flower. Soon after, while topping rushes in the Orchard Meadow, my Son swiped the Iris clump. I waited months to see if it would recover. Luckily, for me, it did produce some flowers in 2009.

Plate 44
1. Iris pseudacorus L. –
Yellow Iris
2. Sparganium erectum L. –
Branched Bur-reed
3. Polytrichum commune L. –
Common Hair-cap Moss
4. Ranunculus penicillatus (Dumort.) Bab.
– *Stream Water-crowfoot*

The Branched Bur-reed grows along the ditch which feeds into the pond. One day I happened to mention, quite casually, that the pond and ditch had dried up. The ditch had silted up at the far end diverting the water along another route. Next day, shock, horror, I learnt that the pond had been dredged out with all the mud thrown back onto the bank. Here again I was lucky that one or two of the Branched Bur-reeds escaped the digger bucket.

In spite of vague feelings of paranoia, I didn't protest. Stewart has enough to cope with, running the farm, without his Mother having a tantrum.

The Common Hair-cap Moss was growing on a damp, densely shaded bank. I didn't set out to record mosses, but this one was distinctive and I felt it added something to the arrangement of water plants.

While searching, underwater again, I was surprised to find the Stream Water-crowfoot growing in fast flowing water where a stream meets the main river. It has only submerged leaves, which I had to keep floating in a dish of water to work out the structure.

June 2009

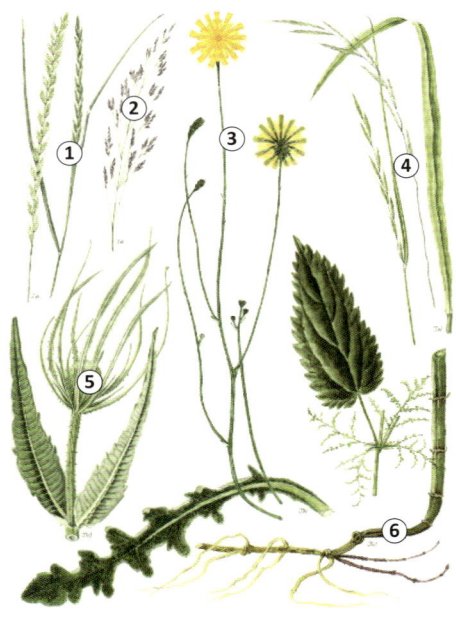

Plate 45
1. **Elytrigia repens** (L.) Desv. ex Nevski – *Common Couch*
2. **Agrostis stolonifera** L. – *Creeping Bent*
3. **Hypochaeris radicata** L. – *Cat's-ear*
4. **Brachypodium sylvaticum** (Huds.) P. Beauv. – *False Brome*
5. **Dipsacus fullonum** L. – *Wild Teasel*
6. **Urtica dioica** L. – *Common Nettle*

This Couch Grass, or Stroil as it is known locally, was growing on the road verge above the retaining wall where I had found the Maidenhair Spleenwort. I went down to the road early one morning to put out my black re-cycling box and noticed the smell of newly mown grass. The council contractor had been there ahead of me and trimmed the verge. It seems to be an occupational hazard, that what the botanical artist earmarks to paint, is either cut down, dug up, or eaten, before it can be painted.

The nettle is dioecious, having male and female flowers on different plants. It tested my powers of observation to the limit, even with the hand lens. The Jury is still out as to which this is, but I am leaning towards female.

The pond 2007 before dredging...

and 2010 after dredging.

June 2009

Plate 46
1. **Epilobium tetragonum** L. – *Square-stalked Willowherb*
2. **Epilobium parviflorum** Schreb. – *Hoary Willowherb*
3. **Epilobium montanum** L. – *Broad-leaved Willowherb*

Willowherbs thrive in the damp moor ground and in my garden!

For a long time, the Willowherbs were a complete mystery. I noticed that those in the moor were the same as those in the garden. So, from the seedling stage, I followed their progress in my borders. I painted the lower sections first, concentrating on the leaves and stems, followed later by the flowering sections. These showed the distinctively shaped stigmas. In this plate, the two sections are not intended to fit together, as there is a lot of plant in between. In the end I felt the long period of observation had paid off and I experienced a real sense of achievement. Needless to say, as soon as I finished, I weeded the border before the seeds flew everywhere.

June 2009

Plate 47
1. Ulmus minor Mill. **Ssp. angustifolia** (Weston) Stace –
Cornish Elm
2. Rosa canina L. –
Dog Rose
3. Potentilla reptans L. –
Creeping Cinquefoil

We lost most of our elms to Dutch Elm Disease. They re-grow from suckers, only to succumb again before reaching any size. The disease killed a long avenue of the trees lining the farm lane. We had them felled and sawn into planks, some of which were used as Yorkshire boarding on a cattle shed. One I saved as a reminder. I chiselled out the farm name, painted the letters black and fixed it on the grassy bank at the entrance. We still have a few very large elms which escaped the disease. They have a broad, rounded canopy, unlike the Cornish Elms, which are more fastigiate. I think they maybe Wych Elms.

The Dog Roses are always a joy. They proved tricky to carry home without losing their petals. It was a toss-up between painting the flowers or the rosehips. In this case, the flowers won. Plants have several periods of growth, of interest to the artist, and it is difficult to choose which to portray. If I was painting for the Eden Archive, I would show both flowers and hips.

July 2009

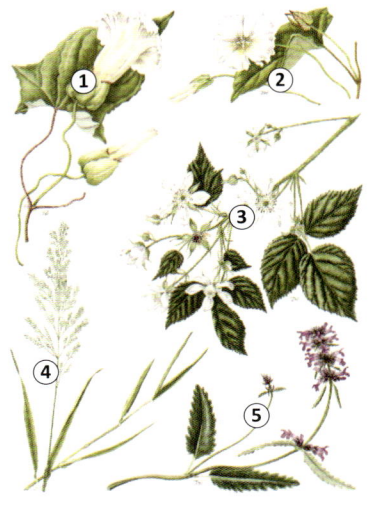

Plate 48
1. **Calystegia sylvatica** (Kit.) Griseb. – *Large Bindweed*
2. **Calystegia sepium** (L.) R. Br. – *Hedge Bindweed*
3. **Rubus** agg. – *Bramble*
4. **Holcus mollis** L. – *Creeping Soft-grass*
5. **Betonica officinalis** L. – *Betony*

The learning process continued right to the end. I learnt the difference between Hedge Bindweed and Large Bindweed. In the latter, the bracteoles are inflated and overlap, hiding the sepals.

I learnt that this bramble is one of around 100 to have been recorded for Cornwall. It may be a member of the section corylifolii.

I learnt to differentiate between Yorkshire-fog below and Creeping Soft-grass another one known locally as Stroil – meaning toil. Distinctive features of the latter are the very hairy nodes. This grass brought my total of grasses up to twenty two.

July 2009

Plate 49
1. Lonicera periclymenum L. –
Honeysuckle
2. Ligustrum vulgare L. –
Wild Privet
3. Rosa arvensis Huds. –
Field Rose

As I wandered about, incidents from my former life as a herdswoman came back to me.
In case I have given the impression, thus far, that farming is all grief and disappointment, this anecdote may go some way to redress the balance.

In the Cows' Moor, where the Field Rose and Wild Privet grow, is a level plateau of drier turf. Cows invariably choose this spot to calve down.

On one occasion, the newborn calf (above) tottered to its feet, took a step or two backwards and slithered down the bank into the ditch. On my next regular check, I found it standing in a few inches of water looking bewildered. Prudence, the calf's dam, looked down anxiously. After manhandling the calf up onto level ground I put it to suck. This manoeuvre is always fraught with uncertainty and entails much or little to-ing and fro-ing before the teat is in its mouth and it takes a swallow of the first milk or colostrum. It is absolutely vital that a calf gets a good quantity of this in the first few hours to protect it from infections. Once it had 'got the message', there was no stopping it, until, replete, it lay down to sleep, the cow relaxed and peace was restored.

July 2009

Plate 50
1. **Hypericum pulchrum** L. – *Slender St John's-wort*
2. **Valeriana officinalis** L. – *Common Valerian*
3. **Scrophularia auriculata** L. – *Water Figwort*
4. **Scutellaria galericulata** L. – *Skullcap*
5. **Lotus pedunculatus** Cav. – *Greater Bird's-foot-trefoil*

This Slender St John's-wort was one I had overlooked previously, but I had been waiting two years to paint the others. While aware of them in the background, others had taken priority. They all like wet conditions. As well as being much taller and straggling, the Greater Bird's-foot-trefoil differs from the common one in having a hollow stem. If any flowers were threatening to go over before I had time to paint them, I made sure I at least had a drawing. I found the best way to identify a plant was to draw it. This made me really look at it. So often before, I had given a plant a cursory glance, and named it, only to be proved wrong later. The Skullcap favours the wet ditches and was one more of those treasures which I had completely overlooked through the years.

July 2009

Plate 51
1. Filipendula ulmaria (L.) Maxim. – *Meadowsweet*
2. Circaea lutetiana L. – *Enchanter's-nightshade*
3. Epilobium hirsutum L. – *Great Willowherb*

The Meadowsweet and Great Willowherb like their feet in the water and heads in the sun and grow well in the swampy area on the Cows' Moor. This Great Willowherb is probably the easiest of the willowherbs to identify.

For variety, I showed the underside of some leaves. The veins are often raised up, casting shadows, and the surface is often matt, without the highlights found on the upper surface. In the case of the Enchanter's-nightshade, I just outlined one pair of leaves, so as not to obscure the delicacy of the flowers. It is a shade lover and thrives where a stream flows past a great oak in the Cows' Moor.

July 2009

Cattle escape the sun in this shady corner of the Bullocks' Moor.

Plate 52
1. Mentha x verticillata L. –
Whorled Mint
2. Eupatorium cannabinum L. –
Hemp-agrimony
3. Cirsium arvense (L.) Scop. –
Creeping Thistle

I believe this Whorled Mint is a cross between Corn Mint and Water Mint. It was abundant in the Robin's Meadow. Although small, this meadow yielded a surprising number of species, some found nowhere else in the moor. The what, why and where continued to intrigue me, inviting a lifetime of study and interest.

The Hemp-agrimony grows in the very wettest spots. It proved to be one of the worst for wilting before it could be drawn, let alone painted. I had even abandoned it the year before because of this, but now it was crunch time and it had to be done.

The Creeping Thistle can be invasive in pasture fields, but is checked somewhat when a field goes into the arable stage of its rotation. Ploughing is not an option in the moor. Here the thistle is confined to the drier areas. The wetter parts are left to the Marsh Thistle, L.

August 2009

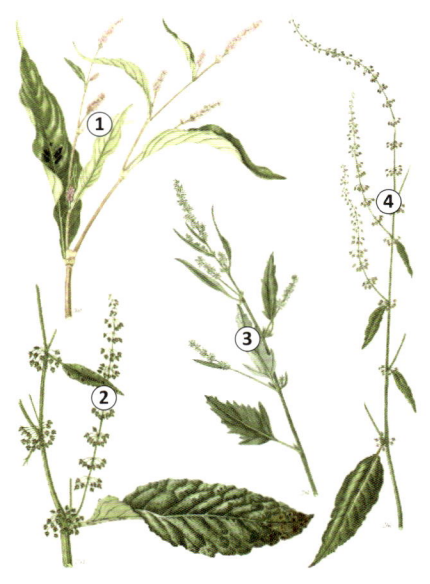

Plate 53
1. Persicaria maculosa Gray –
Redshank
2. Rumex obtusifolius L. –
Broad-leaved Dock
3. Atriplex patula L. –
Common Orache
4. Rumex sanguineus L. –
Wood Dock

As I neared the end, I couldn't put off the docks any longer. Under the hand lens, their seeds are magical. It proved beyond my skill to do them justice life-size. An additional spur to the completion of this project was a request by the Committee of the Eden Project Florilegium Society to present my florilegium at the Annual General Meeting in January 2010.

To accompany my commentary, I wanted to project the images onto a screen. With this in mind, I called in reinforcements, in the shape of my Daughter, Christine, and Grandson, David. David was very patient with his computer-illiterate Granny and soon had them photographed with his digital camera and put on disc, complete with common and Latin names.

Cattle are now housed in winter, unlike those below.
Bullocks' Moor, circa January 1969.

The meeting was postponed until February, owing to the harsh weather. Finally the day came. The plants had been painted. The words had been written. My presentation was very well received. So, a big "thank you" to all the members for their unstinting praise. If I was describing David's contribution to the success of the presentation in football parlance it would be 'The Boy Done Good'. His help has also been invaluable in the design of these pages.

August 2009

Plate 54
1. Mentha aquatica L. –
Water Mint
2. Senecio aquaticus Hill –
Marsh Ragwort
3. Cirsium palustre (L.) Scop. –
Marsh Thistle

So, to the final plate. Throughout this two year project I have been conscious of Mally looking over my shoulder - metaphorically speaking - keeping me from giving up. I thank her for instilling in me a little of her high standards and dedication.

The 29th July 2009 marked the centenary of the publication of Frederick Hamilton Davey's 'Flora of Cornwall'. As I put the finishing touches to my own 'Flora', I paid tribute to his great achievement 100 years earlier. I hope my book will add to the wealth of knowledge already gathered on the Natural History of Cornwall.

If enjoyment of the illustrations and text is an end in itself, that is fine with me. If, in addition, any reader is inspired to emulate it, that is even better. One doesn't need the good fortune to be in possession of a 30 acre plot. Many other areas are both suitable and accessible. Roadside verges, waste ground, church yards, public parks, sports grounds, gardens and riverside walks all have their own unique collections. If painting is not for you, there are other formats in which to create a record of a specific location.

The wild flower walk through the Luxulyan Valley was a good example of what I mean. Between the village and the railway embankment was a very small rough corner, with so rich and diverse a collection of plants that it simply cried out to be recorded. Only stop and look closer and the most unprepossessing plot will be transformed into a place of unique beauty and enchantment.

The end . . . of the beginning
At least ten different brambles
have been found on the moor . . .